A Randonaut Chronicles

By

Satiety McCollum

Table of Contents

Table of Contents Cont'd

Introduction

In case you haven't heard of it, there's a phone app out called Randonautica by Randonauts Co. It's available for both IOS and Android.

It's a game where you think of something you'd like to manifest. Then, with that intent in mind, you click the begin button and it scans the area for points of unusual energy amounts and gives you coordinates to a location for you to explore. It works with Google Maps so you can have easy directions to the destination point.

Here's what their website says:

https://www.randonautica,com

"The Randonautica app was created to encourage users to venture outside of their day-to-day routine by using a quantum random number generator to derive a coordinate to journey to. The app was developed by the global movement, The Randonauts. The phenomenon has taken the world by storm and there are millions of Randonauts exploring their surroundings in nearly every country."

It's a great way to get out during quarantine times, and often it takes you places in your own area that you've never been to. It came out during quarantine, but since it took four years to develop a lot of people are suspicious of the app, and here's why.

First, the user has a choice of getting a location as an anomaly, a void, or a power location. Many Randonauts believe that choosing a void location means it will be a negative experience and choosing anomaly will give a positive result. Not so.

It says in the app that a void is a setting that chooses locations that aren't close together. And anomaly setting means locations where there are clusters of locations. So remember, voids are not negative in Randonautica.

Secondly, it's rumored that Randonautica took so long to develop because they had to hire secret workers around the world to hack the app user's phones and set up the pins and finds according to their intent.

Many people that use the app have noticed something else that a lot of them have in common; they get followed. It even happened when this author used it. The followers usually have a silver or white rig (different kinds but usually silver or white) that follows the users beginning at the destination points when they leave.

They make sure they are seen, as they flash their brights and honk while behind the randonaut. They follow for a certain few miles, then turn off and disappear. Some randonauts have stopped and tried to confront the rando-stalkers, but they always take off.

Often users are directed to places where they find such odd items that it makes one wonder if someone isn't somehow listening on the user's phone and then going there ahead and planting items. Like anything else, and people being human like they are, there are skeptics and tricksters in any field.

Worth Investigating

There are a lot of people trying to get to the bottom of this app, even resorting to questioning the makers, Auburn Salcedo and Joshua Lengfelder.

There are YouTubers spending months doing nothing else but Randonauting all over the US and Canada, and trying to catch the followers and learn more. Some of them are CJ Faison, Omar Mendz, and Jaskinho, and they've even played it together for weeks.

If this app works the way it says it does, you could manifest anything you can think of, within reason, which can be a scarey thought. Thoughts are real things, not an intangible string of words that happens to us. We create them, we put our energy into them when we think the thoughts.

In the nature of this world, like attracts like, so if there is a lot of negativity and dark thinking, that's what will be attracted to the thinker. It's why people always preach peace and love, so those thoughts will surround us puny humans.

Anyone can manifest anything if they put enough energy into it, Randonauts just use the app to take them where there are energy anomalies to do it. It's a good experiment to see if these high points make it easier to manifest things and so far the experiment has been a success, most of the time.

One only has to look at YouTube.com to see hundreds of videos people made of themselves playing Randonautica. Some people are better at manifesting than others, and the ones who can really focus on their intent are the ones who seem to have the most intense adventures.

There are those who use the intents 'death', 'horror', 'satan', 'evil', etc. and that's exactly what they find, in some way. Not to say that everyone with these dark intents has something bad happen, but it happens too many times not to mention, and that's what this book is really about.

Chapter 1

A Few Tips to Play

Randonautica has rules, easy rules that aren't hard to follow. One of them is to ***bring a trash bag with you and pick up any trash at the pin (location).*** Many Randonauts don't even remember this rule, but it's a good one, and if people randonaut just to clean dirty places, that would be very cool.

Before the stories you're here to read are revealed, it's a good idea to know some tips because I know some of you will download the app right away. And that's fine, just be safe, and don't forget your trash bag to clean up your destinations.

1. ***Don't go alone.***
2. Don't go at night unless your intent is creepy or ghost-based ***AND*** you're not alone.
3. Don't trespass, a lot of people have been shot at while trespassing.
4. Take/wear clothes and shoes appropriate for weather and terrain.
5. Bring water if you're going for hours.
6. Don't take anything but pictures and trash from locations.
7. This app can empty a gas tank easily, make sure you're gassed up. You can make sure your locations are close or spread out by setting the radius in the app,

8. Always bring a flashlight and a camera, document the crazy stuff you find.
9. Always bring latex gloves, you never know what you may be touching.

Chapter 2

About Your Intention: Make it Clear

There are those that say the Randonautica app didn't work for them. One example is Stacey from Portland, who said she used the intent 'anomaly'. Their coordinates led them down a trail in the woods to a meadow where everything was green but one bush, which was covered in pink flowers.

She didn't specify what kind of anomaly to manifest, so her anomaly was a plant in full color in the midst of ever-green, non-flowering plants.

Being specific with your words is important for this, among other reasons. Her idea of an anomaly was something wrong or that doesn't work. She didn't stop to think that it also means something that's other than expected, or unlike the others. The flowering bush was definitely not like the other things around it, in fact, the other things weren't even blooming plants.

Try to think of words that closely describe your intent and say them so they can only be interpreted the way you mean them to. But, keep an open mind. Sometimes an intent might be unfruitful but the Randonaut was shown something really cool or unusual.

Another user, Tom in Alaska, used the intent 'riches' and the app took him to an area where millionaires live. He found riches, but they belonged to the people living in those mansions. To find money for himself he should say something like, ‘cash for me’, ‘jewelry for me’, etc.

It doesn’t mean you can have whatever valuable you come across, depending on the location, of course. It simply allows you to manifest and find things. Although, if the intent was gold it might lead you to a sandy beach and you could potentially find a ring someone lost there. Just don’t take someone else’s property, even if you manifested it.

Your intent and concentration are key to this app working. You can play it without an intent, too, but it’s more fun if there’s something that needs to be found. Focus is difficult if you’re driving, so a good practice is to sit in the car a moment to concentrate and focus before getting out to explore. And, be careful. Old buildings may not be safe or legal to explore, but many times you can get permission from private property owners.

Most of the following events were experienced by the author, however, others have contributed their experiences as well.

For the contributors that do not want their name published, a fictitious name will be substituted. I cannot prove or disprove their stories, but they still want their stories to be told. Some of them have been edited.

Chapter 3

Intent: A Surprise

Driving to our destination seemed like a great idea. We'd chosen a void and it gave us a location 13 minutes away, with a power of 4.5 and a radius of 26 meters.

The road was pretty empty of traffic, being out in the country towards the mountain. It was sunshining after a full day of rain the day before and the leaves on the road were drying out.

We drove as far as we could to our location, but we had to walk through the woods about a mile to get to it. My daughter found a safe place to park, so we concentrated on our intent, which was 'a surprise' before getting out and making sure we had our cameras.

When we entered the woods from the trail it was noticeably darker, and the sound of the wind blowing across the tops of the evergreens made it seem kind of creepy.

It was a nice walk, and wildlife was everywhere, birds, squirrels, chipmunks, picas, and black bear, though we didn't see any bears. Just their scat and claw marks.

I looked at the phone and our pin was close, so we began looking for something on the ground or in a tree or bush.

I kept hearing a noise that sounded like a creek in the distance, so we went that direction to find it. Our quest to find it took us far off the trail, and I was wondering if we'd remember the way out. My daughter had been in the US Army and she could always find the way home, lucky for me.

As we got closer to the sound, it became clear that it was not a creek, and there was no body of water around. The noise now sounded like static, or white noise. We pushed on, listening for which way to go and looking ahead for a path.

My daughter spotted something pink not far ahead, so we aimed for it and tried not to smash forest plants as we went.

To our surprise, we came upon a place where it looked like someone had come to spend the day. A transistor radio was hanging on the broken stump of a low branch on a tree, off station but the volume was high, and making the noise we heard from so far away.

The pink was a teddy bear that laid on a blue and white flowered baby blanket spread out on the ground. Next to that was a gym-sized bag that was overflowing with baby pajamas and an empty baby bottle. It looked like we'd just walked up on someone, but there wasn't anyone around.

We turned off the radio and called out hello, but we never got a response. We walked around the area searching for someone that might be hurt or maybe they took the baby for a walk and would be back soon. We waited around for about an hour when the radio turned back on and turned up all the way.

My daughter and I looked at each other with wide eyes, not sure what an appropriate reaction was, but we were startled out of our britches. I ran over and turned it off again, looking around for… something, I don't really know what.

We both thought that was a good time to go and with only a look we took off in the direction we'd come from and walked quickly back to the car.

I still don't know why that stuff was way out in the wilderness, miles from any houses or roads. I still can't explain the radio that turned itself on. It's one of the older radios that the same knob turns it on and controls the volume, so the knob had to be turned all the way for it to play like that. Now I wish I would have checked it for batteries.

Maybe we stumbled upon a ghost's recreation day in the woods, or maybe it was the spirit of a traveler of long ago. Whatever it was, it sure was weird and we have to go back. But, next time, it won't be a 'surprise', as was our intent.

Chapter 4

The Smoke a Bowl Ghost

We went to the edge of town to get a location because when we get one in town, we get residential areas and places where we can't trespass. At the edge of town we got a location 6.1 miles, or 13 minutes away. We set our intent to be something abandoned.

It led us to a road through the forest where all the homes are a good half mile apart. We came to a point where we had to get out and walk from the road to the pin. There was an overgrown driveway so we walked up it to find our location,

The pin was to our right, so we stepped off the driveway and made our way to the location through ferns, bushes and stickers. As we neared the pin we saw a run-down shack that we thought was a tool shed, but when I looked inside I saw old counters and cabinets and remnants of broken furniture inside. One wall was completely missing, so we walked around to it and entered the small ruins.

There was nothing out of the ordinary to find, but as soon as we entered, I noticed a change in atmosphere. It felt heavy and sad, and looking around in the little shack made me feel real sorrow. My eyes teared up and there was a lump in my throat and it was all I could do to stop myself from bursting in sobs.

The person with me, who prefers to remain nameless, took out her recorder and began to ask questions out loud.

"Is anybody here with us?" there was no response. "Does anyone care to talk with us?" About this time I noticed an old corn-cob pipe on the ground and I picked it up and showed the person with me. "Does anybody want to share a bowl with us?"

A wind suddenly kicked up enough to blow leaves around us, and we could see the meter on the recorder fluctuating. That means it was picking up sounds. She turned it off and rewound it so we could listen to it, and it almost made us wet ourselves.

"Smoke a bowl", and "Where is it?" came through the recorder. We looked at each other in surprise, it was loud and clear. I looked around the small place as if I might see the person talking, but I saw nothing.

The person with me suggested we leave, not being prepared to do paranormal investigating. She carries the recorder in her purse, so that's all she had with her.

We walked down the driveway back to the car and headed home. We were only on the road for about a minute when the person with me said, "Why is this guy riding my ass?" I turned to look back, and sure enough, there was a small white truck with a matching canopy very close to us. The windows were tinted so dark we couldn't tell if there was just the driver or if someone was with him.

“I have to try and lose this guy, he’s making me nervous.” She made the next turn we came to, and so did the truck. She sped up, so did the truck, which began flashing it’s bright lights at us, and keeping pace. “I’m going to pull over and ask what the hell this guy wants.

She pulled over and so did the truck. She got out to go back and talk to them, but they took off, speeding around us and down the street where we saw it turn.

For the rest of the way home I watched for this little truck, hoping it wasn’t following us. It didn’t.

Chapter 5

Intent: Death

This story isn't my experience, it belongs to someone I'll call Doris. It isn't particularly scarey but shows how an intent can be interpreted. Doris wrote:

"I love exploring places, and this Randonautica app was just the ticket for me. My neighbor and I decided to try it out together, and our intent was 'death' – I know, pretty morbid, but we like to ghost hunt, too.

"Our first location took us behind the Walmart warehouse and the huge parking lot was empty. We parked and walked around the lot to see what we could find. On the side of the building there were a mass of feathers spread all over the lot.

“We picked up some of the feathers and looked at them and some still had skin attached. The feathers were from a hawk and a raven. Looked like they got into a fight and the raven didn’t fare very well.”

Doris’ intention was death, but the death they found was not of a human. She didn’t see actual death, but there were remnants of a fight that was likely to the death. Hawks and ravens don’t fight for entertainment; that hawk had to be pretty hungry to go after a bird the size of a raven. Doris stated that there were far more raven feathers than there were hawk feathers, fitting the assumption that tho raven lost the fight.

Chapter 6

Intent: Conspiracy

One Spring day we decided to Randonaut because the weather was starting to be pleasant. We set our intent to controversy and hit the road, before I opened the app. In fact, I don't normally open Randonautica at home because I don't know if someone hacks the phones and locations and all the other rumors going around.

It took us down a country backroad for a long way until we reached a little town we never knew was there. I won't say where because I don't want anyone to go there and party or vandalize the place, but I will say it was central Oregon.

Our pin was inside an abandoned building in the center of a large empty lot and it looked like all the windows were broken out. It wasn't hard to get into the place, and then it didn't take long to realize it was once a hospital.

There was a few tables, a bed, and lots of peeled paint everywhere. It was decaying and well on it's way to falling down. We were very careful to step where it was safer and we found our way to some stairs. We went up to the next floor and found it consisted of a network of hallways lined with doors to small rooms. We'd found the patient's ward.

Trying to think of what kind of conspiracy could involve a hospital in a small town, I could hear noises in other places. In the hall I heard sounds coming from a room, and when I went into a room, the noises were out in the hall.

I got an idea and went into a room and stood still to simply listen to all the sounds. Then, in a sickly voice, I said, "Nurse?" then louder, "Nurse?" My partner in the hall recorded what we both heard next.

Someone, a woman, said, "I'm coming!" from somewhere down the hall. We looked at each other and knew each other had heard it, too. It was confirmation to something that was crazy to experience and that nobody

else would believe if there wasn't
witness proof.

The hair on the back of my neck stood on end, and all I could think about was getting out of there before the 'nurse' made it to that room. We took of, trying to be careful and fast at the same time.

Once we were outside it felt safer and we slowed down. It's funny that mere light can make us feel safer, even in the same place that scared us out.

As we sat in the car to catch our breath, we chatted about our intent being 'controversy' and how we found something else. Then it occurred to me; there's been a controversy almost as old as mankind over whether ghosts are real or not.

I believe we did find our intent, but did we manifest it? I think I'll have to do it more before I can make a qualified decision about it. Next time, I'll try to manifest something I can take home with me. I also think we should come back with the intention of ghost hunting.

Chapter 7

Intent: Something Creepy

This story came from someone who we'll call Alex, who doesn't want his name used because when he goes Randonauting he calls in sick to work and doesn't want to be caught. Rando on, young Alex!

"We were excited to use the app because I first downloaded it at work and had to wait until I got off. My buddy and I made up the intent of 'something creepy' and it gave us a location down by the Columbia river to a forest service trail, where we had to walk another 1.1 miles. Hoping the trail goes that far, we got out our backpacks and headed into the woods.

“At first, the trail paralleled the road, but then it curved right and uphill. The further into the forest we went, the darker it seemed like it was, but it was early in the day. As expected, the trail ended, but the app said we still had a ways to go, so we kept going.

“We came to an opening in the woods that looked like someone used to dumped their garbage. On closer inspection, it looked more like an animal had gotten into some trash and went through it there. Some of the trash had large teeth marks in it, making me think it was a bear.

“The rules say to clean up the places we go to, so we did, but we weren’t quite to the pin point, yet. We hung the trash bag where we’d see it on the way back, so we didn’t have to carry it.

“We finally arrive at the pin, and there’s nothing but forest in every direction. We start looking around, and even split up for a while, but we found nothing.

“We could hear a creek in the near distance, so we decided to find it and have a drink and snack before we head back. The creek was at the bottom of a ravine but there were big rocks up where we were, so we sat on those and drank our waters and ate.

"While sitting there, we were discussing our intent and how we may have misinterpreted it somehow. Or, maybe we didn't concentrate hard enough to manifest anything. Just when our mouths were full and we weren't talking, we heard a deep, throaty growl come out of the woods.

"Both of us froze. My partner was the first one to be brave enough (or scared enough) to start putting his stuff away, and I did the same. We high-tailed it in the direction we'd come from and didn't stop until we hit the forest service road.

"My friend and I stopped there to catch our breath and get a drink, and we couldn't help but talk about it. The growl didn't sound small, and I could believe it came from a bear. That is, until this happened.

“We heard the growl again, but this time it turned into a roar. Then another one on the other side of us, and then one up ahead. We were surrounded and we could hear something crashing in the woods, not too far away from us.

“Whatever it was, it was big, judging from the way large bushes and small trees were falling. Then, we heard loud cracking noises in the woods, and a weird whooshing sound, and then there was a tree falling on it’s side. It was a big, mature conifer that was obviously still alive, and it broke and cracked off branches on it’s way down.

“When it hit, we could feel it in the ground, the vibration buzzed all the way to where we were and it stunned us both. We stood there and stared at it until suddenly, there was another, longer growl that sounded like it was right behind us.

"We took off and ran to the highway and I was so glad to find my rig. I had to sit in it and collect myself, staring at where we'd come out of the woods.

"I don't like to admit it, but I was shaking so bad it was hard to steer, and neither one of us spoke the rest of the way home. In fact, we've never spoke of it to each other again. It's hard to believe, and I'm a "have to see it or I won't believe it" kind of guy.

"Now, I'm certain Bigfoot is real. Is he creepy, like my intent? Nah. I'm kind of fascinated and I think I'll go back with a camera some day. Although I didn't manifest my intent, I did find another adventure in the bank while using this app, so I'll try it again."

Chapter 8

Intent: No Intent

It was a cold day, and though it hadn't snowed since the day before, there was a dusting on the ground. Driving wasn't a problem because the roads weren't frozen.

We decided we'd go with no intent, just to see what we'd come across. This time, it gave us coordinates that were in a suburban area.

I usually choose a new location when it's in town because Randonautica often takes us to residences and buildings we can't get into. But, since we didn't have a specific intent, we went for it.

It brought us to a fairly rich neighborhood I'd never known about before. We drove by huge mansions with gated estates and landscaped driveways.

We came to the pin and it was in an open lot with trees, like a small forest park. We parked and got out and began walking into what looked like a few acres of woods. The trail we were on didn't seem to end, we kept walking and walking much farther than it looked.

After about half an hour of walking we came upon a photo of a teenager nailed to a tree. As we looked around, there were more photos on more trees. They were laminated to protect them from weather.

We wondered if these were missing teens from the area, or from anywhere, and did they go missing here in this park, or did they go missing elsewhere? Who put all these photos up? So many questions came to our mind.

Deciding to keep walking, it seemed like we walked another half an hour without seeing the end of the park. It was very strange because it did not look that big, and it's in the middle of a neighborhood. We decided to turn around and go back to the car, and we came to the photo trees quickly. Maybe we hadn't walked as far as we'd thought? Then we come out of the forest within a couple of minutes. Or, did we?

Had we really come out in a tenth of the time it took to get in there? Looking at the time, we'd been in the forest almost two hours, but it took mere minutes to backtrack. It doesn't make sense, and we couldn't figure it out.

Two days later I'd gone to the post office to mail a package, and I casually looked on the board with all the missing person photos. I was surprised to see most of the kids I'd seen in the pictures on the trees. I looked at their specifics and they didn't go missing from that forested park.

I still don't understand what happened with time and the small park that never ended. Maybe a glitch in the simulation, as my partner said. We will go back one day and investigate that.

Chapter 9

Intent: Something Red

It was raining and that made it hard to be motivated to get outside and walk around. I wanted to go, but I don't like being wet and cold. I drove to my friend's house to pick her up and we set our intention to 'something red' and got our location point from there.

Six miles to the north was the outside edge of town, so we weren't sure if it was a residential area or not. When we'd arrived, we found that it was older homes with acreage, so there were houses, but not close together.

We drove for what seemed like too long for a six-mile drive, but I think that was because of all the turns and twists of the road that made us go slow. Hearing my phone finally tell me our destination was nearing made me feel a small charge, excited to find something and explore.

Coming up on the pin I looked ahead for a road or something that we'd have to walk, but in double-checking the app I saw it was right next to the road. There was a clump of brush over-growth that was so big we couldn't see past it until we got there.

I slowed way down to look for something when we passed that bush clump, and I was thoroughly jazzed to see what we found.

It was a ranch-style house that sat back off the road, and it was painted bright red. The curtains were red, cars in the driveway were red, the mailbox was red, and the flowers in the beds were red, and they had a Japanese cherry tree with dark-red leaves.

These people really liked red, apparently, and it satisfied our intent.

Chapter 10

Intent: Beauty

We'd gone to visit friends down south where the landscape is a desert. It gets so hot that nobody has lawns, everyone uses a variety of decorative rock. The land was flat and it seemed like you could see forever the sturdy, stiff plants that can grow wild in such harsh conditions.

Our friends wanted to try out Randonautica for the first time, so of course we were happy to oblige them. They own an SUV with a hatchback, so we loaded that with food and drink and headed out.

Deciding as a group to use the intent 'beauty' we followed the directions given us. Ten miles in almost a straight line from their house, we had to get out and walk. On the way it had started to rain. When we got there, a torrential downpour raged through the area and then was over in about five minutes, so we waited in the car.

Everywhere there was a dip or low spot in the terrain instantly filled with water and new little streams developed everywhere. It was surprising that the arid land didn't soak it up immediately, but it was too much too fast, I guess.

When the water had subsided and the sky cleared, we got out, and it didn't take the sun long at all to evaporate what water was left. As we walked through the freshly shocked desert, we saw something incredibly beautiful. Something I'd read about but never seen with my own eyes before.

Every rough and stickery bush, shrub, ground dweller and thistle grew a color. Plants were blooming almost before our eyes. An hour later and all of them were in full bloom. There were reds, yellows, pinks, and still the dulled greens and greys that were the plants themselves.

Then, as if that weren't enough, flying insects and bees seemed to appear out of nowhere. They were going from bush to bush and buzzing around our ears, seemingly trying to get the pollen and

nectar in the short window of time
before the flowers all close again,

It just developed and gave an
unexpected beauty that I could see,
hear, and feel all around me. It seemed
to have the same effect on the people
that live there. It was almost magical.

Chapter 11

Intent: Spooky

Next time we Randonauted we drove 60 miles south before getting our location. In a small town on the side of the highway, we pulled over to open the app, getting a location that was on the other edge of this tiny little town. It was 2.5 miles but there was almost no traffic, so it didn't take long. Our intent was 'spooky'.

The location was an old cemetery (perfect for our intent) just off the road and surrounded by trees so that it looked round. It had an old wood fence that made it seem if we'd gone into another time, back in time.

We walked around and looked at the graves, and some of them were downright picturesque, and we took a lot of pictures. The cemetery was well groomed and it was a lovely place. We spread out a blanket and sat do eat and drink, and it started to get dark. I wasn't afraid at all, it was like sitting in any park, until dark. Then, it was like no other picnic I've ever had.

At first I thought I heard dogs yipping in the woods around us, but after a while I could tell they weren't dogs, they were people. We listened, but couldn't understand any words they used.

Then there was movement in the woods, lots of movement. We could see between the branches in the darkness what looked like shadow people running the entire circle of the graveyard. We could see them run from shadow to shadow, disappearing or becoming part of them as they circled the little cemetery. I mean, a lot of people, maybe fifty, some running one way and the rest running the other way, all of them yelling something.

The really spooky part came when we realized that to get back to the car, we had to walk through the parade of shadow runners. We packed up our stuff and began walking back across the lawn, feeling like we were being watched by everyone.

As soon as we set foot on the driveway, all the voices and runners were gone. Disappeared, it was suddenly like any normal night in the graveyard.

On the way home we talked about getting what we asked for, because it was exactly that. Randonautica did not disappoint. In fact, it was so spooky, we can't wait to do it again.

Chapter 12

Intent: The Unknown With A Place Where Ghosts Party

When quarantine opened up a bit in the fall my friend and I drove across the country to see friends. We drove to Manhattan, Kansas and made reservations at their Motel 6. I'd stayed there before and it's nothing to write home about.

You walk into the tiny lobby and are greeted ten minutes after you get there because the concierge is on his phone. There is a small cushioned bench you can sit on, and there's a vintage end table with shelves that are stuffed with books and board games.

When he finally paid attention to us, he went through the motions and spoke in a monotone that told me he didn't want to be there. Ignoring him, we got our key and went through the hallway to our room.

Our window was at parking lot level, so when we looked out we saw the tail end of cars parked there. We had everything; two queen size beds, a full bath, heat/air, a hairdryer; cverything but a coffee pot. Of course, I asked for one.

I called my friends and we made arrangements to meet for breakfast in the morning before we started

Randonauting. That before we had to get back in the car. Our TV didn't work, and we were told the cable in the whole building was out temporarily.

Remembering the games I'd seen downstairs, I mentioned them and then went to chose one to play. It felt weird walking into the quiet, empty little lobby, where the kid stood at his post but didn't seem to notice me, again. I went to the game table and sat on the floor to look through them.

The games seemed to be all mixed together with some parts in each box. I tried making whole games in the right boxes, but none of them had all its pieces, except one; a Ouija Board. I hadn't played with one of those before, and it was the only form of entertainment I could find.

I wondered what my traveling partner would think of it as I walked back to our room. When I brought it in, she took one look and said, "Cool, a Ouija Board!" She took it and opened it up on her bed.

It was still daylight, so we turned off the lights and just used the window light. It's a good thing the instructions were printed on the box because neither one of us had used one before. We took our places on each side of the board and carefully put our first two fingers on each hand lightly on the planchette.

I asked if there was anyone there that wanted to talk to us, and then we waited. Nothing moved, so then I asked if this room had any spirits in it, and again, nothing happened, at first. Then, slowly at first, the board began sliding around under the planchette, spelling out words that way instead of moving the planchette.

First, the board moved so that the planchette was right over the word "Yes" in the upper left corner of the board. As soon as the board started sliding, my friend and I looked at each other as if to say, is this how it works?

I read it out loud and slid the board back and put the planchette back to center for my next question. "Did you die in this room?" once again the response was slow in coming, but the board slid to make the planchette rest on "No". It seemed pretty weird because I've seen Ouija Boards on TV and

YouTube, and the like. Its always the planchette that moved.

My friend wanted to ask a question. “Do you want to hurt us?” I shot her a look, not sure if I wanted to know or not. This time the board didn’t take it’s time and moved to put the planchette over “No”.

“Are you moving it?” my friend asked me. I had both hands on the planchette, there was no way I could be doing it, and I could see it wasn’t her doing it, either. But, I guess we had to make certain.

We asked it a bunch of questions, like, how will we die, how many kids will I have, just silly stuff like that. She started yawning around 11pm and I was tired from the drive, too, so we put the board away and crashed for the night.

Yes, it's Haunted

But, we didn't sleep well. The first thing was a party going on in the she room next to us. They were laughing out loud, the music blared, and it sounded like someone fell on things when I woke up. My friend was already awake.

"Do you hear that?" she asked me. I got up and called the front desk, and a woman answered; she must be the night shift. It was 3am. I reported all the noise next door and she said she'd take care of it right away. We waited, but half an hour later the party was still loud.

I called the desk again and the same woman answered. I told her the party was still raging, and she said this:

“I’m sorry, Ma’am, but there isn’t anyone in that room. I checked after you called the first time, and there’s nobody on that lower floor but you.” So I asked if it could be coming from the room above us, and she said the only rooms that were full were ours, and two rooms way down on the end of the upper level.

I thanked her for her time and was confused. How could there be nobody in that room? I stepped out into the hall and I could still hear it, so I went to the door of the room on that side and knocked really hard, like cops do. The room instantly went silent. Suddenly I could hear the ice machine down the hall and the air conditioning kicked on, it was so quiet. I waited, but nobody answered the door, and not another sound came out of there.

I went back to my room and crawled in bed, But I was awoken not long after that by the bathroom light that kept turning on and off. Not wanting to get up again, I just yelled, “Oh for Christ’s sake, knock it off!” and to my surprise, it stopped. I did sleep the few hours I had left, but I woke up thinking about that party next door.

Glad to Leave, Glad to Stay

We got ready and packed up our stuff and headed out to meet my friends for breakfast. I hadn’t seen them in two years, so it was a great reunion and we were excited to go Randonauting. After breakfast we piled into their Suburban and talked about what our intent would be. We decided on using 'the unknown'.

My friend's husband was driving, and we'd gotten a location 6.1 miles away. We all concentrated on our chosen intent as well as chit-chat catching up. We got on the highway my friend and I had come in on, and we went about five miles before we had to take a right.

This particular right turn was made of overgrown gravel and went downhill and disappeared into a stand of trees. He slowly took the turn and we were all quiet and watching out the window.

We drove by what looked like a flooded forest; I was later told that the area floods every year and the water recedes to normal every year.

He stopped at our location and we all got out to look around. My friend reminded us of our intent, ‘the unknown’, so we all tried to see what could possibly by unknown in a half-flooded forest.

Finding Unknowns?

There were still plenty of dry places to drive and walk on, and I caught a whiff of skunk. It wafted around and then disappeared as quick as it had come. I started to look around for an animal and walked into a sunny patch where there weren’t any trees.

The skunk smell enveloped me in plants as tall and taller than I am. It took me a minute to notice the leaves as I searched for a skunk, and I realized I was in a big patch of hemp plants. It was in full bloom, so it was really stinky like a skunk. I knew it grew wild all over the state but I'd never stumbled across it. It was actually a pretty plant.

My Kansas friend called out to us to come see what she'd found, so we all went to see. She'd found what looked like an old mine shaft that had a wooden, barely-standing guard rail around it so nobody fell in. It wasn't otherwise marked, so it was a hole in the ground with an old wood ladder inside it.

It looked very inviting to adventurers, and I'm an adventurer, but I'm also smart. I could die if I went down there, but man it was cool.

After some time in the sun, we all got back into the Suburban and went to my friend's house. We all had a great time exploring and even they said they'd never been down there before, so Randonautica scored again.

It wasn't until much later that I remembered the Ouija Board and the events of the night before. My traveling partner and I told our sides of that story over drinks, and we found out that motel is rumored to be haunted.

I'm not sure if we manifested 'the unknown' or not, but persomally, I did learn things and have exposure to something previously unknown to me.

Chapter 13

Watchers, Weirdos, and Rando-stalkers

This is what happened to YouTubers Jaskinho and CJ Faison of Faison Nation and Motivated Eyewear and Merch.

Both of these guys have been doing Randonautica videos for a while; Jaskinho has been playing non-stop for seven months (at the time of this writing) straight. CJ has also done many Randonautica videos in between his haunted and paranormal videos.

These guys made friends and Jaskinho began traveling to PA where he and CJ took a trip Randonauting across the country. They're trying to figure out how the app works, and every time they're followed by a white rig that flashes it's lights, honk its horn, and rides their tails.

For a while in the west, they kept meeting up with or being watched by local police. Once they were in the Nevada desert where the town was no more than a few shacks and RVs gathered together, with houses every now and then.

The only cop in that town parked where he could see them and just watched. If they moved, he moved, too. They weren't doing anything wrong, but felt eerie and finally moved to an area where the cop wouldn't follow.

Jody Dean, creator for the channel Hunting the Dead on YouTube, has done many Randonautica videos with his wife, whom he calls his Pinkie Pie (a pretty woman who sports bright pink, long hair).

Because of Randonautica use, they've attracted a Randostalker, who's been inside their cars, put trackers on Jody's new truck, left morbid drawings at each Randonautica location they go to.

There is one video where he went Randonauting with Omar of OmarGosh TV on YouTube, and used the app on Omar's phone to get their location, and still the Randostalker beat them there and left more drawings for Jody. He also sent Jody a text saying that he saw him with Omar.

That's pretty freaky and brings a whole 'nother level of creepiness and mystery to this app.

These guys aren't going to find the answers they're looking for by playing the game repeatedly. They need to do some other kind of digging. However, they put their heart and soul, and a lot of their time into these adventures.

There are two Tik-Tok videos that have become world famous, and it's not for any small reason. Two separate instances where the teens were looking to manifest 'death', and one girl found a man who'd been shot laying on the street, and the other was a group of teens that found a suitcase on the edge of a river, and it had human remains in it.

One can find a plethora of manifested Randonauts creating adventures on YouTube, Twitter and TikTok, and likely other sites online.

Chapter 14

Intent: Something we'd Never Seen Before

24-year-old Emily in the center of Oregon, sent me this story.

"We tried Randonautica and didn't manifest anything at first, but we kept trying it and eventually it finally happened. We set out with the intent of finding 'something we'd never seen before', and we practically chanted our intent on the way.

"Where I live is out in the sticks and sometimes we don't have cell service. We went out Barnes Road, a twisty, narrow old highway with what looked like an ancient rock guard wall on the steep side.

"We reached our pin and stopped on the side of the road and decided to get out and walk around. Looking at the ground and the ditch, we didn't realize we were coming to a driveway.

"We heard a lady at the residence screaming for help like her life was being taken, so we ran up the driveway. The screaming was coming from a small barn, so we ran inside to see what the problem was.

"There was a lady with her arm up to her shoulder in the rear of a horse. I stopped because I didn't know what was going on there! She saw me and waved us over, sayng she had to turn the foal around, it was breech and she needed help.

"We hurried over and did what she told us, which was mainly keeping mama horse calm. The lady took her arm out of the horse's... uh, rear (not the rear but, you know), and little front feet came out after.

"When the birth was over, she rubbed the newborn roughly with a towel and the mama licked it. The little baby looked right at me, and I almost felt a connection.

"The woman explained that her husband was taking a nap and she thought she'd check on their pregnant mare. When she went out she found the mare struggling to give birth to a breech fetus, or he was backwards.

"She needed help and was trying to scream loud enough to wake her husband when we came by. We spent a couple of hours there before we walked back to the car, and we felt like we'd experienced a miracle that day. I think we glowed! We manifested our intent because we definitely saw something we'd never seen before!"

Chapter 15

Randoblockers

This is not a single person's story but several people's (including mine) because it's something I'm experiencing and hearing from other Randonauts. There are some places that the app does not work, and we're perplexed as to why.

Are there some places that have technology that automatically blocks the app from working? Or is it that the makers just don't put points in certain places?

More than once I've been near the post office (and once in a hospital waiting room) and the app told me there are no points in the area, please move to another area, or something along those lines.

I just watched a video by OmarGoshTV on YouTube where he took his family to Disney World in Orlando, FL. They tried to Randonaut inside the park in different areas, but to no avail. It gave him the same message I got.

A friend of mine was inside the Mormon Temple in Lake Oswego, Oregon, tried to use the app in the massive place, but she also got the message about moving to try again. When I first heard this, I wondered if it was all the gold and marble that coats the temple, but after similar stories happening in mundane places, I no longer think that.

Now it'll be interesting to see if it works at colleges, courthouses, and other federal and local entities. I remember being in a church in Manhattan, Kansas, where nobody had cell phone service inside because it was a church/bomb shelter and it was built with something that blocked the signal.

Because of that, I do know without a doubt that there are some places where the Randonautica app won't work due to things put in place long before the app was invented. Could this be the reason for all instances? I guess we'll have to keep trying it to find out.

Chapter 16

Intent: Run!

Having watched a ton of Randonauts on YouTube I have noticed that every time the 'Nauts are approached or find another person in the area, they hide and/or run from them. I've always wondered why, and in some of their live chats I've asked them. I'm told by more than one Randonaut that it's because you never know who is a weirdo and who isn't. if you never meet them, you never have to find out.

I'm a social person, and although I have seen many weirdos on these YouTube videos, I still give a person a chance to give me something to judge, before I do.

Given, some of these Randonaut videos have had (seemingly) dangerous experiences, like a clown with a knife is waiting and chases them off. Or there's people standing in a small circle, in the middle of the forest at night that turn and walk to you when they realize you're there. I mean, lots and lots of weird stuff. Anyone would run from them.

However, I've met some of the nicest people while Randonauting. We often use the intent 'haunted' or 'ghosts' and three times (not in a row) the app gave us the same address.

The first time we went there, it was abandoned and we couldn't get into it. The second time, there was workers there and code compliance notices, but the workers wouldn't let us in while they worked, for safety reasons. The third time, we found a family had moved in.

I really wanted to know about this place and I wondered why we were brought there three times in as many weeks. I couldn't just leave without finding out something. I went up to the door and knocked, making sure I was six feet from the door when they answered.

An older gentleman answered and asked if he could help me. Just then a feeling of awkwardness washed over me and I felt my cheeks get red. This was so out of the ordinary, that I'll bet they talk about it for a long time to come.

I introduced myself and asked him if he'd heard of the phone app

Randonautica, and he said no. I explained the app and showed it to him and told him that I just couldn't help it, I had to ask. Is his house haunted?

He laughed out loud and said no, that he'd lived there 30 years and never noticed anything out of the ordinary, and his family were all still alive. You can imagine the conversation this sparked, and I don't even know how long I was on that porch, but it was fun and I'm glad I met him. Not like we'll keep in touch, it was just a pleasant time.

It happened again at another address when our intent was 'something magical' and we'd been given this one four times. At the moment, we stopped in the street to calculate another location and while we were waiting for the app to respond, an older couple came out onto their porch and waved at us.

I got out and explained what they were doing, and having not heard of Randonautica before, they had a lot of questions and seemed genuinely interested. I told them we got their address four times when using the intent 'something magical' and our exact pin was actually in their large backyard.

They said it was a usual backyard, nothing magical, but if I wanted to take a look I was welcome to. I did. As I mentioned, their backyard is quite large, maybe a triple lot in that residential area. We walked around the yard looking at everything; the dirt, plants, grass, trees; everything.

After a good twenty minutes I had an urgent need to use their bathroom, and they were gracious enough to let me. I don't think I appear as someone who rob them or something. When I came out of the bathroom I looked at their home – beautifully appointed with original artwork everywhere.

I began asking about this piece and admiring that piece, and some of them she brought my attention to. It surprised me that probably half of her art collection was free or super cheap because the maker didn't value it (as an artist, I completely understand this, as pieces I made that I disliked the most are the ones that people raved over or I sold for the most money). There was also her own art – beautifully detailed sculptures in different mediums. I was very impressed.

We ended up staying about an hour and even had coffee with them, and now she and I are good friends who stay connected through our arts. I didn't realize it until some time afterward, but making a new friend at my age is magical. So I guess we did manifest our intent.

Other times we weren't always alone at a Randonautica location, and many times we didn't interact with anyone else while we were there. I've never been around someone that put so much fear in me that I'd can my plans and run because I saw another person. Give me something to be afraid of, and I'll be afraid of it, but the mere sight of a person doesn't make me bolt. But then, we haven't come across any clowns with a knife, either.

As I've said, I've met some super nice people using this app, and maybe that's part of ITS intent? I don't know, hmm.

Chapter 17

Intent: Bumps in the Night

Sometimes Randonautica finds you a home to rent, too… or, not.

On our way to our Randonautica location (our intent was 'bumps in the night'), we passed a cute house that had a "FOR RENT" sign on it. We stopped, wrote down the number, and two weeks later we moved in. It was smallish, but our kids weren't living at home anymore, so it was enough room for us. The rent was crazy low, considering the size of the property it sat on. It had a cute yard and the house was painted blue with white trim, and gave me a generally happy feeling.

Except for one thing; there were no kitchen counters or cabinets. The landlord said he was waiting on them to come in and they were late, so we lived without counters for a while. Night stands and tables became the norm, and we had a sink and appliances.

I worked every day until 1pm, and I began noticing things weren't the same as when I left in the morning. It was always something small, like a butter knife in the sink, or the TV remote in a different spot. I had a large dog who was very protective of me, so I didn't think she'd let anyone in and there was no fear there.

We were there about a month when I noticed that when I came home every day, the heat was already turned on and the house was warm. At first I figured my husband had come home for some reason and turned it on for me, but it turned out not to be him. Not too long after that, I noticed things missing from the fridge, like leftover lasagna AND the bowl it was in. The dish eventually showed back up – in the sink...

And all that whole entire time, I was also hearing noises that sounded like they were in the attic. This house didn't have the kind of attic where someone would store things; it had no floor or walls or even lights. Whenever my husband had to go up there he had to be careful where he stepped so he didn't come through the ceiling. I couldn't imagine any animals living in fiberglass, or at least that I know of. It makes me itch just to think of it.

I thought, maybe the new house is haunted? I've lived in a haunted house before, and it's a classic symptom when something you use all the time disappears, and also when it shows back up (sometimes years later or only in photos) in an obvious place. It could explain things that went missing in the kitchen and later showed up in the sink.

The noises upstairs could have been wind blowing through the old and unweather-ized building, but many times there was noise and no wind, so that didn't explain it all. Mice, maybe? Even if they didn't live in fiberglass, they may use the structure as pathways across the house.

Being the ghost adventurer that I am, I got out my mic and my recorder and cameras, and I did an investigation on my home, the whole home, and I didn't find anything out of the ordinary.

Underneath the house only had a crawlspace, but no basement of any kind. I looked for, and found, the way to get into the attic; it was in the hallway between the bedrooms and it was the kind where you pull the door down and stairs come out when it opens. I went to get a flashlight, and when I did, I heard a bunch of shuffling noises come from the attic, like I'd scared a family of racoons or something.

Back up the stairs with a light, I shone it into the darkness on one side of the house, then the other, as the stairs seemed to be in the center of the house. I went all the way up and shone my light on the other side of the house, where I saw plywood sheets laying on the rafters like a floor.

Careful to step only on wood, I made my way over and shone my light around the area. I found bedding and a pillow, some containers with remnants of our food in it, and other things that made me sure that the animal in our attic was of the human kind.

The moment I realized that, fear shot through me and it almost hurt. I hurried back to the stairs and pushed them up as I closed the door.

The same thought ran through my head and out my mouth repeatedly, “There’s someone up there, there’s someone up there, there’s someone up there,”. I wasn’t realty sure what to do, call the police, leave and wait until hubby came home, call a friend or neighbor over and chase him out with me… I was frantic, I was shaking, I could hardly push the numbers to dial the phone to call hubby home right now.

He came home and called the police before even looking up there. We waited downstairs and it seemed like forever, but was only about 20 minutes, but the whole time we listened intensely to any little noise.

The police came and took my report, and they went upstairs and looked through his belongings finding a state ID, and when the third officer (of three) saw it he said he knew who the person was. The officer said he isn't a harmful person or a thief, he's just a local homeless drunk. He hadn't seen him around for several months, and maybe it's because he'd been staying in my attic.

I thought about all the time I spend at home alone, and I wondered if he listened to conversations or watched me go about my day down here. I now knew who was eating sandwiches and leftovers and why my dishes disappeared and reappeared. I wasn't crazy after all (and now my husband knows it, too), but the best part is knowing my new house is NOT haunted

Randonautica, you did me a solid!

Chapter 18

Intent: Missing People

YouTuber Jaskinho (Yas-keen-yo) and his buddy Chris have spent the last seven months doing nothing but Randonaut adventures.

In December, 2020, the app took them to an abandoned mill that was down river from a trailhead. The log at the trail head showed that someone named Blane Taylor entered the trail but she never logged out, making them wonder if something happened to her.

They spoke to the owner of the property next to the mill and he was very rude to them and told them they could go in for a price, but he didn't think they had enough money to see what was inside that old mill. Jaskinho offered him $100 and the old man said he wanted more, so they said forget it and left, but not before the old man spit on their car..

They heard screams coming from the direction of the old mill, and in the log it said that's where Blane was headed. They wondered if it was her that they heard screaming.

Making their way to the mill (after crossing the river) they found a bag with the initials "BT" on it, some photos of someone's family, and other items. So they looked around to see if they could find more, while they heard many odd noises that sounded like there was someone else in the old mill with them. But, they never found anyone.

They returned another time, and this time they didn't bother with the owner next door. Jaskinho was concerned about the girl, Blane Taylor being there possibly injured or dead/dying, especially after finding more belongings that were marked "BT".

There were no signs of her that they hadn't already found, but they kept looking around. Jaskinho couldn't stop thinking about what may have happened to her, and a search gave no help.

Many times Randonauts have found evidence of crimes, kidnappings and murder weapons. They always turn the items in to the local authorities, not wanting to be caught with them or caught leaving them. It's the right thing to do.

If anyone knows a person with the same name, ask them if they've been to the old mill, and get some details to post on Jaskinho's IG account or YouTube channel.

Chapter 19

FAQs

update: I still have not heard back from the creators of Randonautica. It's been a week, but I will keep waiting.

On the Randonautica website, there are some good questions with answers. One of them is, ***Will anything bad happen if I use the app?*** The creators say to go with an open, but positive mind set. You know the old saying, if you look for bad you will certainly find it.

This makes sense on several levels. The power of suggestion is a strong tool performed by the mind. We can literally think the world we want and if we believe it enough, we can manifest it. Research has shown that positive thinking can change a person's entire outlook and the world they live in.

Another question is ***Why can't I walk around and use the app while on foot?*** The websites response is, "If your goal is to find completely new places that you didn't know about before, you should take into account the inherent determinism of the macro-world. Any decision that we make, as a rule, is the result of certain associations and logical processes, whether conscious or subconscious." I'm not sure if the question was answered, or not.

"...How can you say that Randonauting isn't part of the pattern?" The website answer is:

"It is predetermined, the only thing that is nondeterministic is the random location. In theory, your fate can predetermine you using

Randonautica, but not visiting those exact places.". Makes sense.

"What should I do at the point?" The app says to explore! If it takes you to a place you're familiar with, look for things that are new or changed, and think about your thoughts on the way there. It's possible you manifested something other than your intent.

"Does Randonautica collect user information and/or data?" The app says: "The application does not collect user data. The generated points (but never your starting point) are stored as anonymized information, with no connection to you or your device. We utilize GPS only for your starting location and never run this permission in the background."

"Does Randonautica go against my religion?" The website says: "You may have heard that the app can be used for spiritual and conscious awakening. While this may be the experience for some, you do not have to use the app in any way that contradicts your spiritual beliefs. If you still have concerns, we recommend that you consult leaders of your faith.

"What is a reality tunnel?" Randonautica says, "We define a 'reality tunnel' as the deterministic path that your life is on. Reality tunnels are influenced by factors that determine the relative frame of reality for a particular person. For example, perhaps subconscious influences on where you end up in the world, and what you take notice of while you are there."

More books by Satiety McCollum

All are available on Amazon and Kindle!

Your Inner Artist: Bring it Out

1 5 projects with step-by-step instructions.

https://www.amazon.com/db/B08NS7GT7

Gift-Worthy Goodies: Quality Gift for a Few Bucks

Quality gifts that can be made for a couple of dollars or your SNAP benefits.

https://www.amazon.com/db/B08LR3BHXR

An Ambiguous Living

A small collection of my insane poetry.

https://www.amazon.com/db/B08M87RVYZ

Conversations with Two Eight Seven

The story of an Alaska family who rented a haunted house.

Https://www.amazon.com/db/B08M87RVYZ

Ghost House on Park Avenue

The longer version of the above book with lots of extra stories and happening descriptions.

https://www.amazon.com/db/B08P3QTGGR

How to Write a Good Essay

A Learning Work Booklet study aid

https://www.amazon.com/db/B08M7J3SWL

How to Write a Poem

A Learning Work Booklet study aid

Https://www.amazon.com/db/B08M8DDGK
W3

Ghost House on Ketchikan Creek

Two teens in Alaska find a haunted house and end up learning how to live with them. Based on the true story, "Conversations with Two Eight Seven".

Https://www.amazon.com/db/B08P3QTGGR